BookLife
freedom
Readers

BIRD
PREDATORS

BY MIGNONNE GUNASEKARA

BookLife
PUBLISHING

©2022
BookLife Publishing Ltd.
King's Lynn
Norfolk PE30 4LS

ISBN: 978-1-80155-139-7

Written by:
Mignonne Gunasekara

Edited by:
Shalini Vallepur

Designed by:
Amy Li

BookLife
freedom
Readers

A catalogue record for this book is available from the British Library.

All facts, statistics, web addresses and URLs in this book were verified as valid and accurate at time of writing. No responsibility for any changes to external websites or references can be accepted by either the author or publisher.

CONTENTS

MEET THE PREDATORS

Welcome to the world of predators. Predators are animals that hunt other animals for food. They come in many shapes and sizes, but they all have something in common – to the prey that they hunt, they are terrifying!

4

In this book, we will be looking at predators that are birds. They might look beautiful, but don't be fooled — they rule the skies as well as the roost.

RED KITE

Red kites live in woodlands and other open areas. Many red kites were killed by humans in the past, and the species nearly went extinct in the UK. This means that there were almost no red kites left in the UK. However, they are now recovering.

Red kites are scavengers. They eat the remains of animals that are already dead – this is called carrion. They sometimes hunt small animals, such as rabbits, but red kites usually eat whatever prey they can find.

GREAT SKUA

The great skua is a large seabird. It has been known to fly angrily at anyone that gets too close to its nest. Great skuas eat fish, carrion, and smaller birds such as puffins.

The great skua is also known as bonxie. It is also sometimes called a 'pirate of the sea' because it steals food from other birds. Its sharp beak and talons help it to catch its prey.

BARN OWL

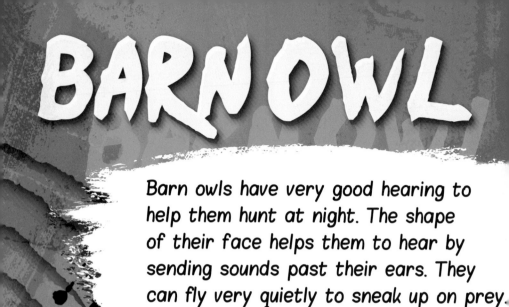

Barn owls have very good hearing to help them hunt at night. The shape of their face helps them to hear by sending sounds past their ears. They can fly very quietly to sneak up on prey.

Barn owls eat small mammals such as voles and mice. They bring up pellets from their mouths. Pellets are made of parts of prey that cannot be broken down in the stomach, such as bones and fur.

PELLET

COMMON
KINGFISHER

These small, colourful birds can be found
fishing near rivers and other slow-moving
waters. They mostly hunt for small
fish and shrimp,
but they
also eat
insects.

Common kingfishers hunt by sitting on perches near water, where prey is easy to spot. They dive into the water to catch prey and bring it back to their perch to eat.

BALD EAGLE

Bald eagles belong to a group of birds known as sea eagles. They have very good eyesight and can see prey from far away. They have sharp talons to help them hunt, and sharp, hooked beaks to rip into food.

Bald eagles use their talons to grab fish out of the water. They eat a lot of fish, such as salmon. They also eat carrion and steal prey that other animals have killed.

GREAT WHITE PELICAN

Pelicans are some of the largest birds on Earth. They are known for the stretchy pouches under their bills, which they use to scoop fish out of the water. They also have webbed feet that help them swim.

Great white pelicans usually fish in groups. They can fly long distances to look for food. They swim together and push the fish into one area, then scoop them up to eat.

PEREGRINE
FALCON

Peregrine falcons can be found everywhere, from cliffs by the sea to tall buildings in cities. A peregrine falcon's main prey is other birds such as pigeons, but they also eat bats.

Peregrine falcons have pointed wings and sharp talons that help them hunt. They hunt by diving at their prey while flying. They can reach speeds of over 300 kilometres per hour while diving. They grab prey out of the air with their talons.

COMMON KESTREL

Common kestrels can be found in many habitats. They eat small mammals such as voles, mice and shrews. In towns and cities, common kestrels may find it easier to eat birds than mammals. Sometimes they might eat insects and worms.

Common kestrels have an interesting way of hunting. They can stay in one place in the air while flying. This is called hovering. Hovering makes it easier for the common kestrel to see and catch their prey.

SPREAD YOUR WINGS

Congratulations, you met the predators. They are all very fierce and some of them are huge, too. Let's see them stretch their wings and fly. Which bird has the widest wingspan?

A wingspan is the distance between the tips of each wing when they are stretched out. A bald eagle's wingspan can be two metres wide. The kingfisher has a wingspan of around 26 centimetres.

QUESTIONS

1: **Where do red kites live?**

2: **How do peregrine falcon's hunt?**
   a) By flying below their prey
   b) By diving at their prey while flying
   c) By using stones and sticks

3: **Can you name two animals that the common kingfisher eats?**

4: **Why is the great skua called a 'pirate of the sea'?**

5: **Which is your favourite predator and why?**